Links: Twentieth Century World Hist
Series Editor: Robert Wolfson

C000246016

Conflict in the Middle East
Israel and the Arabs

GCSE Edition

Michael Scott-Baumann

Edward Arnold
A division of Hodder & Stoughton
LONDON   MELBOURNE   AUCKLAND

Acknowledgements

The publishers would like to thank the following for permission to reproduce copyright illustrations:

John Frost's Historical Newspaper Service and
   The New York Daily News, Cover.
The Mansell Collection Ltd., p. 5t.
BIPAC, pp. 5b, 6, 15, 16, 26, 29, 39, 41, 42t,
   42b.
The Imperial War Museum, p. 8.
BBC Hulton Picture Library, pp. 9, 10, 19,
   22b.
Associated Press, p. 12.
Popperfoto, pp. 14, 18, 20, 22t, 34, 37.
Camera Press Ltd., pp. 25, 36t, 36b.
The Evening Standard, p. 31.
CAABU, p. 32.
Embassy of the Arab Republic of Egypt, p. 35.
United Nations Information Centre, p. 40.
Orde Eliason, p. 44.

© 1984 Michael Scott-Braumann

First published in Great Britain 1984
Second edition 1987
Second impression 1989

British Library Cataloguing in Publication Data
Scott-Baumann, Michael
   Conflict in the Middle East: Israel and
   the Arabs.—GCSE. ed.—(Links)
   1. Jewish-Arab relations
   I. Title   II. Series
   956 DS119.7
   ISBN 0–7131–7626–1

All rights reserved. No part of this publication may be reproduced or transmitted in any form or by any means, electronically or mechanically, including photocopying, recording or any information storage or retrieval system, without either the prior permission in writing from the publisher or a licence permitting restricted copying. In the United Kingdom such licences are issued by the Copyright Licensing Agency, 33–34 Alfred Place, London WC1E 7DP

Printed in Great Britain for Edward Arnold, the educational, academic and medical publishing division of Hoddar and Stoughton Limited, Mill Road, Dunton Green, Sevenoaks, Kent by The Bath Press, Avon.

Series Preface to GCSE editions

The GCSE editions are designed for students following GCSE courses in Modern World History. They have been revised to take account of GCSE syllabuses and assessment objectives. Each topic has been treated in sufficient detail to prepare candidates for the written paper, while also providing appropriate material for coursework assignments. A range of source material is incorporated into each text and the exercises have been devised to develop students' skills in relation to the following GCSE assessment objectives: 1) to recall, evaluate and select relevant knowledge and deploy it in a clear and coherent form;   2) to use and understand the concepts of cause and consequence, continuity and change, similarity and difference;   3) to look at events and issues from the perspective of people in the past;   4) to use the skills necessary to study a variety of historical evidence by comprehending and extracting information, by interpreting and evaluating (for example, distinguishing between fact, opinion and judgement, detecting bias and identifying gaps in the evidence), and by comparing different types of historical evidence and drawing conclusions from such comparisons.

Title Preface to GCSE edition

Why has Israel fought four major wars with her Arab neighbours in 25 years? Why has it proved so difficult to make a lasting peace in the Middle East? These are two of the questions which this book attempts to answer. The GCSE edition traces developments in the Middle East right up to the US bombing raid over Libya in 1986. Inevitably there will be events and opinions which do not receive a mention, but it is hoped that this book will explore most of the causes and consequences of the conflict. Above all, the book aims to develop an understanding of the many different viewpoints on this most complex of contemporary problems.

Michael Scott-Baumann

Contents

Note: The words which appear in **bold type** in the text are defined in the Glossary on page 47.

1

'Next Year in Jerusalem' – The Jews

From about 1000 BC, the Jewish people lived in the land of Palestine (see map 1). In the first century AD, Palestine was ruled by the Romans. In AD 70 and again in AD 135 the Jews rebelled against their Roman rulers. Roman soldiers crushed both revolts, sacked the city of Jerusalem and expelled the Jews. Many thousands fled to neighbouring countries and over the next 200 years they settled in every part of the Roman Empire except Britain (see map 1). Many became merchants and farmers, bankers and craftsmen. Some became wealthy and even gained important positions in the governments of the new lands they lived in.

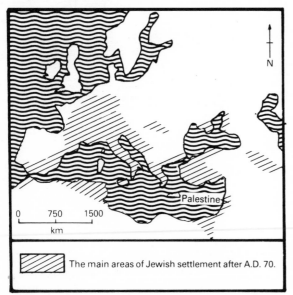

The main areas of Jewish settlement after A.D. 70.

Map 1   The main areas of Jewish settlement after AD 70. By AD 300 Jews had settled in all parts of south and west Europe except Britain. In the Middle Ages they were expelled from western Europe and many settled in Russia and Poland. The settlement of Jews in many parts of the world was known as the **diaspora.**

But they were often **persecuted**, especially in Europe. Almost all Europeans were Christians and they often forced the Jews to live in separate areas. They were not allowed to vote or even to buy their own land. Such anti-Jewish behaviour is known as **anti-Semitism**.

In the 19th century, the country with the largest Jewish population was Russia. When the Tsar, or Emperor, of Russia was assassinated in 1881, there were many anti-Jewish riots. The new Tsar's government encouraged the **persecution** of Jews. **Synagogues** were burnt down, Jewish houses were attacked and thousands of Jews were killed. Many Russian Jews fled to Western Europe and the USA. But even there, Jews found that they were not treated as equals and that they were sometimes suspected of being disloyal or untrustworthy.

In 1896, Theodor Herzl, an Austrian Jew living in Paris, published a book entitled *The Jewish State*. In it he wrote:

Source 1

Are we to get out now, and where to? Or may we remain, and how long? Let us first settle the point of staying where we are. Can we hope for better days? I say we cannot hope for change in the current of feeling. Even if we were as near the hearts of princes as are their other subjects, they could not protect us. They would only feed popular hatred by showing us too much favour.

He said his plan was 'perfectly simple': the Jews were to be granted 'a portion of the globe large enough to satisfy the rightful requirements of a nation'.

A Jew is attacked in Russia in the late 19th century.

We must not imagine the departure of the Jews to be a sudden one. It will be gradual, continuous and will cover many decades. The poorest will go first to cultivate the soil . . . they will construct roads, bridges, railways and telegraph installations, regulate rivers and build their own dwellings; their labour will create trade, trade will create markets and markets will attract new settlers.

For hundreds of years Jews dreamt and prayed that they would be able to celebrate 'The Next Year in Jerusalem'. By the beginning of the 20th century an increasing number of Jews in America and Europe were, like Herzl, demanding a Jewish National Home. By 1914, when the First World War broke out, these people were all agreed that this 'Homeland' would have to be in Palestine. This was the 'promised land', where the Jews (or Israelites) had lived 2000 years before and where some still remained. Most Jews wanted to stay in France, Britain or Germany, or wherever they were living but a small number, especially from Russia, made their way to Palestine. They bought land there and started to farm and build homes. These people and all those

Theodor Herzl.

who believed in a Jewish national homeland were called **Zionists** (Zion is the Jewish word for Jerusalem). Between 1880 and 1914, 60 000 **Zionists** settled in Palestine.

In the First World War the **Zionists** received great encouragement from Britain. In 1917 the British were very keen to bring the USA into the war against Germany. They also wanted the new, revolutionary government in Russia to continue fighting against the Germans. Believing that the Jews in America and Russia could influence their governments' actions, the British declared their support for a Jewish homeland in Palestine.

Their declaration was made in the form of a letter to Lord Rothschild, a leading British Jew, in November 1917. It became known as the 'Balfour Declaration' because it was signed by the British Foreign Secretary, Lord Balfour. For the next 30 years many Jews regarded this declaration as a promise from the British Government to help set up a Jewish state.

Foreign Office,
November 2nd, 1917.

Dear Lord Rothschild,

I have much pleasure in conveying to you, on behalf of His Majesty's Government, the following declaration of sympathy with Jewish Zionist aspirations which has been submitted to, and approved by, the Cabinet

"His Majesty's Government view with favour the establishment in Palestine of a national home for the Jewish people, and will use their best endeavours to facilitate the achievement of this object, it being clearly understood that nothing shall be done which may prejudice the civil and religious rights of existing non-Jewish communities in Palestine, or the rights and political status enjoyed by Jews in any other country".

I should be grateful if you would bring this declaration to the knowledge of the Zionist Federation.

The Balfour Declaration.

Exercises

1 Look at the picture of an attack on a Russian Jew and answer the following:
   (a) How does the artist suggest that the authorities did little to prevent such **anti-Semitic** behaviour?
   (b) Can you think of any reasons why some Governments allowed their soldiers to ignore these attacks on the Jews?
   (c) How was this picture made (for example, is it a drawing, a photograph, or a print)? Who might have made this picture? How useful do you think it is to an historian?

2 Read Source 1 on pages 4 and 5.
   (a) What reason does Herzl give for saying that the Jews cannot expect protection by the governments of the countries in which they were living?
   (b) Why did Herzl think the creation of a Jewish homeland could not happen quickly?

3 Look at the sentences below, then match each sentence in list A with one sentence from list B.

List A	List B
In biblical times the Jews lived in Palestine.	Each year they prayed for 'The Next Year in Jerusalem'.
The Romans crushed the Jewish revolts.	This aimed to win Jewish support.
Most Europeans were Christians and were suspicious of the Jews.	Thousands of Jews fled abroad.
Jews dreamt of returning to 'the promised land'.	**Anti-Semitism** was widespread.
In the early 20th century many Jews wished to see a Jewish homeland established.	In those times they were called the Israelites.
In 1917 the British Government issued the Balfour Declaration.	They were known as **Zionists**.

2

The Struggle for Independence – The Arabs

For many centuries the Arabs have lived in the lands which we call the Middle East. They form the majority of the population and all speak the same language, Arabic. In the 7th century AD most of the Arabs were converted to the religion of Islam. They became followers of Mohammed, now known as Muslims. From their homeland in Arabia, they swept across the Middle East and North Africa in the 7th and 8th centuries spreading their new religion by force. Palestine was one of the countries they took over.

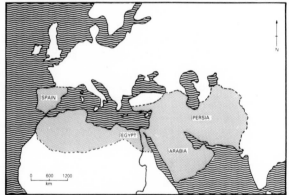

Map 2   The Arab Empire in the 8th century.

In the Middle Ages, the Arab Muslims made important discoveries in mathematics and medicine. Their merchants bought and sold goods in Europe, Africa and Asia, and their lands grew rich. But in the 16th century the Turks (who were also Muslims) conquered much of the Middle East. The Arabs were forced to pay taxes and provide soldiers for their Turkish masters.

In the late 19th century the Arabs tried several times to remove their Turkish overlords. Their aim was to establish Arab rule in the Middle East, including Palestine. In 1914 an Arab writer made this appeal:

Source 2

. . . Arise, O ye Arabs! Unsheath [take out] the sword from the scabbard. Do not let an oppressive tyrant who has only disdain for [looks down on] you to remain in your country; cleanse your country from those who show their enmity [hatred] to you, to your race and to your language.

O ye Arabs! . . . You all dwell in one land, you speak one language, so be also one nation and one land.

Do not become divided amongst yourselves . . .

Exercises
1 Look at Source 2.
   (a) Who is the 'oppressive tyrant'?
   (b) How does the writer think the Arabs should achieve their independence?
   (c) What evidence is there to suggest that the writer does not wish to see several independent Arab nations emerge?

The First World War was a turning point in the Arab struggle for independence as well as in the Jewish struggle for a homeland. Turkey fought on the German side against Britain and her allies. The British were afraid that their supplies of oil from Persia (see map 2) might be cut off by the Turks. So they decided to encourage the Arabs to rebel against their Turkish rulers and seek independence. The British **High Commissioner** in Egypt, Sir Herbert McMahon, exchanged several letters with Hussein, the Sharif of Mecca, an important Arab Muslim leader. McMahon promised that if the Arabs fought against the Turks, Britain would be 'prepared to recognise and support the independence of the Arabs'.

An Arab army was raised and led by Prince Faisal, the son of the Sharif of Mecca. The army blew up Turkish trains and disrupted the flow of military supplies to the Turkish soldiers. The activities of this army are well known because an Englishman, Major Lawrence, who became known as Lawrence of Arabia, fought with the Arabs. In 1918 Faisal and his Arab soldiers were allowed by the British to march in and take over the city of Damascus from the Turks. Naturally they felt they had fought for and achieved their independence from the Turks.

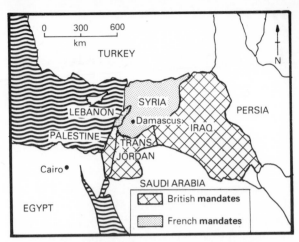

Map 3   The Middle East after the First World War.

mandates over Palestine and Iraq and British troops and their administrators took control of these lands. France was granted **mandates** over Syria and Lebanon and soon sent troops in to gain control.

Prince Faisal (left) with Lawrence of Arabia.

Arab leaders were therefore angered when they heard that Britain and France had secretly agreed in 1916 to carve up Turkey's Arab lands after the war and share them out between themselves. The Peace of Versailles confirmed Arab fears in 1919. Britain and France were given **mandates** or orders to govern certain countries in the Middle East until the Arab people were considered ready to govern themselves. Britain was given

Exercises

2 Under the heading 'The Arabs in the First World War', write out this paragraph, filling in the gaps:

In the early 20th century many Arabs demanded independence from their ____ rulers. In the First World War, Britain was afraid that Turkey might cut off her ____ supplies. The British promised ____, the Sharif of Mecca, that they would support Arab demands for independence if the Arabs would rebel against the Turks. An Arab army, led by Prince ____, blew up Turkish trains and railway lines. An Englishman who later became known as ____ of ____, fought with the Arabs. After the war, however, Britain and France were given ____ to rule Arab lands.

3 (a) Why do you think Britain and France might have made a secret deal in 1916 to divide Turkey's lands between them?
   (b) Britain made promises to the Jews, the Arabs and the French in the war. Which of these people would feel most betrayed? Why?

3
British Rule in Palestine

British troops in Jerusalem, 1917.

In 1917 British troops entered Jerusalem, the capital of Palestine, driving out the Turks. In 1919 Britain was given a **mandate** to govern Palestine. For the next 30 years the British Government was to rule the country. In 1922 the League of Nations confirmed that Great Britain:

Source 3

. . . shall be responsible for placing the country under such political, administrative and economic conditions as will secure the establishment of the Jewish national home and the development of self-governing institutions, and also for safeguarding the civil and religious rights of all the inhabitants of Palestine irrespective of race or religion.

The Arabs of Palestine felt that they had simply exchanged Turkish rulers for British ones. Like the Arabs of Syria, Iraq and Transjordan (the name given to the land east of the River Jordan), they were frustrated and disappointed that they had not been given their independence.

The Palestinian Arabs were even more angered by increasing Jewish **immigration** and the fact that the Jews were buying land in their country. Furthermore, Arabs who had worked on the land were put out of work because only Jews were employed to work on Jewish farms. The Jews only bought land in a few parts of Palestine, but in these areas the Arabs claimed they were being driven out. Their leaders accused the British of being pro-**Zionist**. The British **High Commissioner**, Sir Herbert Samuel, was Jewish. To the Arabs the British seemed to be favouring the Jews.

Ever since the first Jewish settlers arrived from Russia in 1882, there had been attacks on Jewish property and people. In 1921 violence on a massive scale erupted.

The town of Jaffa (see map 4), already famous for its oranges, was a busy sea port. It was different from other Arab coastal towns because it was the main port of arrival for Jewish **immigrants**. Just to the north of the town was Tel Aviv, the largest Jewish settlement in Palestine. In May 1921 an Arab

9

Jewish settlers working on the land in Palestine.

mob set upon the Jews. After two days of rioting, 200 Jews and 120 Arabs were dead or wounded.

The British authorities immediately stopped all Jewish **immigration**. The Arabs were told that only a part of Palestine was to be made into a Jewish National Home. Soon afterwards **immigration** began again, but the British insisted that it would be limited. The Arabs asked the British Government to make Palestine independent as they hoped that the Arab majority would be able to dominate the Jewish minority. When Winston Churchill, a Cabinet Minister, visited Palestine in 1921, a group of Arab leaders asked him to go against the Balfour Declaration and stop **immigration**. Churchill replied:

You ask me to **repudiate** the Balfour Declaration and to stop immigration. This is not in my power and it is not my wish.

The British Government seemed unable to satisfy either Jews or Arabs. The rate of **immigration** slowed down in the 1920s, and yet the Jewish population still doubled in the ten years after the war. By 1928 there were

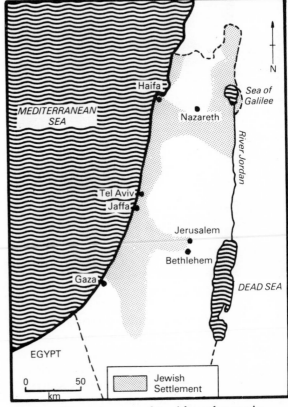
Map 4   The main areas of Jewish settlement in Palestine.

600 000 Arabs and 150 000 Jews living in Palestine. However, the years from 1922 to 1928 were fairly peaceful.

The city of Jerusalem is the Holy City for the Jews but it is also the third most important city for the Muslims. In the 1920s there was continuous tension in the city and some Arab leaders claimed that the Jews intended to take over some of the Arab (Muslim) holy places. In August 1929 large Arab crowds attacked Jews inside and outside the city. The attacks spread throughout Palestine and in four days 133 Jews were killed. During the attacks, 116 Arabs were killed also, mostly by the British police while attempting to stop the anti-Jewish violence.

Jewish immigration . . .

Similar outbreaks, though not so widespread, continued in the early 1930s, especially after 1933. In that year Adolf Hitler came to power in Germany and Nazi **anti-Semitism** drove many Jews out of the country. Thousands fled to other parts of Europe, America and Palestine and by 1939 there were nearly 450 000 Jews in the country. The Arabs were naturally alarmed and attacks on Jewish settlements increased. The investigations of the British Government all came to the same conclusion — the Arabs were afraid of losing their country as more and more of them became 'landless and discontented'.

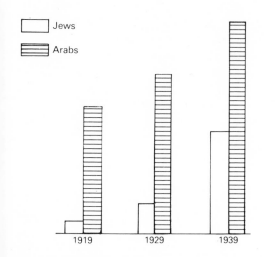

Jewish and Arab populations in Palestine, 1919–39.

The British therefore planned to restrict **immigration** and land sales. This caused uproar among the Jews in Europe and America as well as in Palestine, so the plan was put aside. The British were in an impossible position: if they allowed unrestricted **immigration**, Arab fears and violence would increase, but if they stopped or controlled **immigration**, the world would accuse them of inhumanity, of not caring for the Jews who were being **persecuted** by the Nazis.

. . . and Arab response

In 1936 armed bands, led by local Arab leaders, began to attack Jewish settlements. Within a month, over 20 Jews had been killed. By mid-summer, Palestine was caught up in a civil war which was to last for three years and cost hundreds of lives. The British decided to end the fighting by using troops and harsh punishment. They hanged several Arab mayors and destroyed houses suspected of containing Arab terrorists or arms. The British also helped to organise the Jewish Defence Force, the **Haganah** (which was later to develop into the Israeli army).

At the same time, the British also tried to find a peaceful solution to the fighting although a government report of 1937 stated that co-operation between Arabs and Jews was impossible.

Source 4
(from *Palestine Royal Commission Report*)

About 1,000,000 Arabs are in strife with some 400,000 Jews. There is no common ground between them. The Arab community is predominantly Asiatic in character, the Jewish community largely European. They differ in religion and in language. Their cultural and social life, their ways of thought and conduct, are as incompatible as their national aspirations [as different as their hopes for their nations]. These last are the greatest bar to peace. The War [of 1914–18] . . . inspired all Arabs with the hope of reviving in a free and united Arab world the traditions of the Arab golden age. The Jews similarly are inspired by their historic past. They mean to show what the Jewish nation can achieve when restored to the land of its birth. National assimilation between Arabs and Jews is thus ruled out . . .

The report recommended the **partition** of Palestine into two separate states, one Jewish and one Arab. The Arabs rejected it and the fighting continued. With the help of more troops, better weapons and transport, the British forces gradually regained control of Palestine.

In 1939 the British government gave up all further ideas of **partition**. They declared that they would continue to rule Palestine. War in Europe was approaching and the British feared the growth of friendship between Arab leaders and Germany. Britain needed to keep the friendship of the Arab countries so that oil supplies from the Middle East would continue to reach Britain. The Government therefore published a special report called a White Paper which stated:

Source 5

It is proposed to established within ten years 'an independent Palestine State . . . in which Arabs and Jews combine in government in such a way as to ensure that the essential interests of each community are safeguarded'.

For each of the next five years a quota of 10,000 Jewish **immigrants** will be allowed . . . (apart from a special quota in the near future of 25,000 refugees) 'as a contribution towards the solution of the Jewish refugee problem.'

After the period of five years no further Jewish **immigration** will be permitted unless the Arabs are prepared to acquiesce in it [agree to it].

The Jews were furious.

Jews demonstrate against the White Paper in Jerusalem, 1939.

Exercises

The British and Palestine 1917–1939

In this exercise, you will be examining the reasons why so many Jews came into Palestine between 1917 and 1939 and the attitude of the British to their arrival.

You will need to use Sources 3, 4 and 5, together with the Balfour Declaration on page 6 and the graph on page 11. You will also need a general understanding of events which you will have gained from Chapter 3 as a whole.

1 In what way did the Balfour Declaration and the League of Nations mandate encourage Jews to go to Palestine? (Source 3)

2 Both the Balfour Declaration and Source 3 refer to Britain looking after the Arabs living in Palestine. Copy out those sections of these two documents that state this.

3 (a) How does Source 5 suggest that the British felt, by 1939, that they should do more for the Arabs in Palestine?

   (b) How might a Jew who had gone to Palestine in the 1920s feel about Source 5 if he compared it with the Balfour Declaration and Source 3?

4 Source 4 suggests reasons why the Arabs and Jews were opposed to each other. What are these reasons?

5 'By 1939, the British aim to establish an independent Palestine state ruled jointly by Jews and Arabs stood no chance of success.' Explain fully whether you agree or disagree with this statement.

6 (a) What kind of documents are each of the Balfour Declaration, Source 4 and Source 5?

   (b) What advantages and disadvantages do such documents have for historians?

   (c) If an historian wanted a full picture of events in Palestine between the wars, what other types of sources might he/she consult? Explain your choices.

7 Read the sentences below. Which might have been said by an Arab and which by a Jew? How can you tell?

This is the land God promised to the Israelites.

The British promised us our independence. Now they are our rulers.

Our land is being taken from us. We are being forced out of our own country.

The British are not **impartial**. They are organising the Haganah.

The British are being **anti-Semitic**. They are planning to refuse entry to people fleeing from Hitler.

The British are betraying our people for the sake of oil.

8 *Either*

   (a) It is 1939 and Hassan, an Arab farmer, has just been made landless. He used to farm ten acres of land but his landlord has sold it to a Jewish **immigrant**. He has a wife, Fatima, and four young children to look after. The family decide to move to Jaffa to look for work and somewhere to live. They only have a few possessions and two donkeys on which to carry them. Make the heading 'An Arab explains the problems of Palestine under British rule' and explain the problems which Hassan and Fatima face in Palestine.

   Or

   (b) It is 1939 and Saul, a Jewish business-man, and his wife, Lotte, have recently arrived in Palestine after leaving Nazi Germany. They fled from Germany with only a few clothes and just enough money for the boat trip to Palestine. They are now living with friends in Tel Aviv but are hoping to borrow some money to buy a plot of land. Make the heading 'A Jewish **immigrant** explains the problems of Palestine' and explain the difficulties Saul and Lotte expect in starting a new life in Palestine.

4

The Emergence of Israel

The King David Hotel was blown up by Jewish terrorists.

The King David Hotel in Jerusalem housed the British Military Headquarters in Palestine. It was protected by barbed wire, machine guns and patrolling soldiers. At noon on 22 July 1946, a lorry drove up to the entrance of the hotel kitchen. Men dressed as Arabs got out and unloaded their cargo of milk churns. They rolled them into the building. No one guessed that the milk churns contained high explosives or that the 'Arabs' were members of **Irgun**, a Jewish terrorist group. At 12.37 p.m. the explosion tore through the building killing 88 people, including 15 Jews.

Outrages like this were the result of hatred of British rule which developed amongst the Jews in Palestine. When they heard of the deaths of thousands of Jews in the Nazi Holocaust, **Zionists** began to demand that the Jews in Palestine should be granted their own independent state. They wanted a flag and an army of their own. They wanted a state where the survivors of Nazi Germany could live in peace.

During the Second World War, many Palestinian Jews fought in the British army but after the war they became impatient with British rule. Jewish leaders in Palestine thought the British were stopping them from having an independent state. For this reason, Jewish terrorists began to bomb British army bases, barracks, bridges, trains and railways in Palestine and they attacked the King David Hotel.

Despite such acts there was widespread sympathy in Europe and America for the Jews who had survived the Nazi concentration camps. The large Jewish population in America gave millions of dollars for Zionist leaders and forced US President Truman to put pressure on the British. He said Britain should allow 100 000 Jewish **refugees** to enter Palestine. The British Government refused, claiming it would be unfair to the Arabs. British leaders said it would lead to civil war in Palestine.

The British continued to stop boat-loads of illegal Jewish **immigrants** from landing in Palestine. In 1947, for example, a ship called *The Exodus*, carrying 4500 **refugees** from Europe, was prevented from landing and was sent back to Europe. The British were also exhausted after the war and could hardly afford to keep 100 000 troops in Palestine. After 30 years of trying to solve the problems of Palestine, the British Government announced in December 1947 that it would hand over Palestine to the United Nations.

The Exodus arrives in Palestine carrying Jewish refugees from Europe.

UN partition plan

In November 1947 the United Nations had voted to divide Palestine and set up both a Jewish and an Arab state. Although the Jews only formed a third of the population of Palestine, they were to be given the larger area of land (see map 5) despite the fact that there were many more Arabs than Jews living on that land. The Palestinian Arabs rejected this plan. They did not wish to give up so much land. They felt that the Western powers should find a home for the Jews elsewhere. After all, the Arabs were not responsible for the **Holocaust**.

Palestinian Jews accepted the plan but not all of them were happy with it because many of their settlements were to be included in the Arab state and the Holy City of Jerusalem was to be an international zone. Menachem Begin (later Prime Minister of Israel) announced:

The **partition** of the homeland is illegal. It will never be recognised . . . It will not bind the Jewish people. Jerusalem was and will for ever be our capital . . .

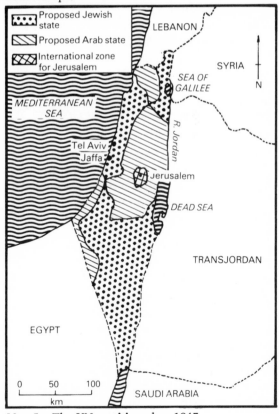

Map 5   The UN **partition** plan, 1947.

15

David Ben Gurion, who was to be the first Prime Minister of Israel, said:

Tens of thousands of our youth are prepared to lay down their lives for the sake of Jerusalem. It is within the boundaries of the state of Israel just as Tel Aviv is.

Fighting between Arabs and Jews increased. There was a bitter struggle to control the roads leading to Jerusalem. Soldiers from Syria and Iraq began to cross into Palestine to help the Arabs, while the **Haganah** organised Jewish defence forces. **Extremist** Jewish groups attacked Arab settlements. They feared the Arab majority in the new Jewish state and hoped to force the Arabs to leave.

Exercises
1 Study the map of the UN Partition plan on page 15. What problems might you expect in a state which is divided into three parts?
2 Why do you think there was so much fighting over Jerusalem? (Look again at p. 11 in Chapter 3).
3 Make a list of the reasons why you think the British decided to hand over Palestine to the United Nations in 1947.

Massacre

The village of Deir Yassin, outside Jerusalem, was the target of a Jewish attack. At 5 a.m. on 10 April 1948, **Irgun** fighters, led by Menachem Begin, advanced on the sleepy village. By noon they had murdered all the inhabitants — men, women and children. This act spread panic amongst the Arabs. A French Red Cross official, who investigated the massacre, wrote:

The press and radio spread the news everywhere among Arabs as well as Jews. In this way a general terror was built up among the Arabs . . . Driven by fear, the Arabs left their homes to find shelter among their kindred [relatives] ; first isolated farms, then villages, and in the end, whole towns were evacuated.

By May 14 1948, when the British finally withdrew, over 300 000 Arabs had fled what was to become the new Jewish state. The state of Israel was proclaimed and immediately, armies from the Arab states of Egypt, Syria, Transjordan and Iraq invaded the new country.

Ben Gurion, Israel's first prime minister, proclaims independence, 1948.

The Arabs of Palestine were disorganised and leaderless and most of the armies from the other Arab states were poorly trained and badly equipped. The Arab Legion from Transjordan, which was the only experienced Arab force, held the Old City of Jerusalem. On other fronts, the Israelis resisted and the United Nations ordered a cease-fire in June. However, fighting broke out twice more and by January 1949, Israel had driven out the Arab armies and even occupied some of the land which the UN had granted to the Arabs (see map 6). In addition, about 700 000 Palestinian Arabs had fled from their homes. Israel refused to hand back the land she had occupied in the fighting, while the Arab government refused to accept that the state of Israel existed.

The development of Israel

The Israeli state had survived its first great test because the Jews had defended it fiercely and successfully in the war. The Jewish soldiers were hardened by their experience in fighting with, and against, the British and, in this war against the Arabs, they were well-led and organised.

The people of Israel realised that they were surrounded by enemies. They were convinced that the Arabs wished to drive them into the sea and would try to attack again. The Israeli army would have to be constantly on the alert. Israeli men were liable to be called up for military service.

The Israeli army also helped to shape the new nation. The Jews of Israel had come from different parts of Europe and America. Between 1949 and 1954 another 700 000 arrived. Most of these came from North Africa

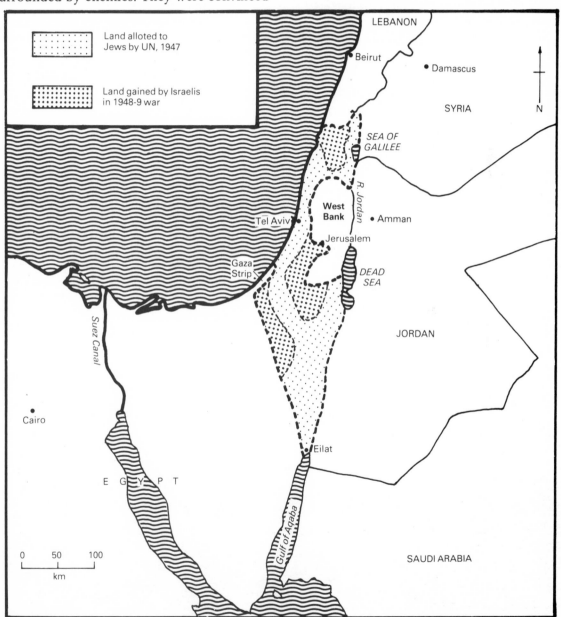

Map 6   Israel and neighbouring states after the 1948—9 war.

and other parts of the Middle East. In the army they all received a similar training, lived together and had to learn Hebrew. So it was experience in the army that helped to make the newly arrived Jews into true Israelis.

Many Israelis went to live and work on **Kibbutzim**. These are large co-operative farms in which all the property and work was shared. Different families ate together and shared living quarters. With financial aid from the USA and Germany, the Israelis irrigated vast areas of desert. They established oil, chemical, shipbuilding and motor industries.

A nation on guard

Israel is a small country and none of the Israelis felt really safe from attack. They feared that the Palestinian Arabs, most of whom had left Israel, would try to win back the lands they had lost. Nearly half a million Arabs had fled to the two areas of Palestine that were not taken over by Israel. These two areas were the West Bank, which became part of the state of Jordan, and Gaza, a thin strip of land which the Egyptians controlled (see map 6). Palestinian **fedayeen** on the West Bank and in Gaza carried out raids into Israeli territory. The Israelis **retaliated** fiercely.

Palestinian refugees walk past Jewish fortifications to Arab territory.

Exercises
4 (a) Why did Jewish terrorists attack the King David Hotel?
   (b) What were their reasons for attacking Deir Yassin?
5 What do you understand by:
   (a) 'The Arab governments refused to accept that the state of Israel existed'?
   (b) 'The Israeli army helped to shape the new nation'?
6 Draw a chart like the one below and complete it to outline why the Israelis won the war of 1948--9.

Reasons for Israel's victory 1948--9	
Israeli strengths	Arab weaknesses

7 Trace map 6 on page 17. Using colours and a key, mark on the seas, rivers, national boundaries and areas gained by Israel in the 1948--9 war. Also mark on the West Bank and Gaza Strip and the cities of Tel Aviv, Jerusalem, Beirut, Cairo, Amman and Damascus.

5

Nasser's Egypt

The Arab states were shocked by their defeat at the hands of the Israelis in 1948—9. It showed how weak and divided they were. It made them bitterly anti-Western. The Arabs felt that the USA had bullied the United Nations into creating the new state of Israel. They suspected that the Western powers would use Israel as a base from which to keep an eye on the new Arab states. Also the Arab governments were not completely independent even after the Second World War. The **mandates** had ended but there were still many Western troops and advisers in the Middle East. For example, in Egypt, which was the most powerful Arab state, there were 70 000 British troops in the Suez Canal area. The Canal was owned and run by the British and French. It was a vital route for oil supplies to the West (see map 7).

Map 7   The Suez Canal oil route, 1956.

A group of young Egyptian army officers were determined to get rid of the British troops and achieve full independence for their country. But first they had to overthrow the unpopular monarch, King Farouk, and his weak, corrupt government. In 1952, after years of planning, they forced the king to give up his throne and took over the government. Their leader was General Neguib, but the real organiser was Colonel Nasser.

Colonel Nasser.

Nasser

Gamal Abdul Nasser and the other young officers agreed to carry out certain social reforms. The most important was land reform. They passed a law which stopped anyone from owning more than 80 hectares of land. The surplus land was shared out among the peasants. They also planned to build a huge dam across the River Nile at Aswan. This would create hydro-electric power for

The Aswan High Dam being built across the River Nile.

Egyptian industry and enable millions of hectares of land to be irrigated.

In 1954 Nasser became President and, after long discussions, he persuaded the British to withdraw their troops from the Suez Canal zone. Britain and the USA still wished to keep on good terms with Nasser. They wanted Arab support in the Middle East against the USSR. They particularly wanted an alliance with Egypt as she was the strongest, most developed Arab nation, and because the Suez Canal passed through her territory. But Nasser wanted Egypt to be neutral and was not willing to join an anti-Soviet **alliance**. He did, however, need arms in order to strengthen Egypt's army. This became very urgent in February 1955 when the Israeli government decided to hit back at Egypt for encouraging Palestinian raids into Israel. Israeli troops attacked the Egyptian Army Headquarters in Gaza and killed fifty Egyptian soldiers. For three days Palestinian refugees in Gaza ran riot and demanded:

Arms, give us arms, we shall defend ourselves.

Even in Cairo, the crowds wanted retaliation.

The Suez Crisis, 1956

In September 1955, Nasser shocked the West by agreeing to buy Russian arms from Czechoslovakia. He said:

I told the British and US Ambassadors last June, that if their countries did not supply me with arms, I would have to obtain them from the USSR. I stated that it was not possible for me to remain silent while Israel imported weapons for her army from several sources and imposed a constant threat on us.

Britain and America, however, thought they could still control Nasser because he depended on them for money to build the Aswan High Dam. Then suddenly, in July 1956, Britain and the USA refused to lend any more money. Perhaps they hoped to persuade Nasser to be more co-operative. Maybe they thought they could force the Egyptians to replace him. But Nasser shocked

the West again. He was not going to be pushed around any longer. He would prove that Egypt was independent now. Before a huge crowd, he announced that the Suez Canal was 'our canal'. Egypt would **nationalise** it and use the profits to build the Aswan Dam. He said that Britain and France could 'choke on their rage'. This daring act thrilled the Arabs in Egypt and elsewhere.

Britain and France were furious. The British Prime Minister, Anthony Eden, was determined not to let Nasser 'have his thumb on our windpipe'. The British and French withdrew their pilots who guided ships through the Canal. But the Egyptians kept it running and the traffic increased.

On October 24 the British and the French Foreign Ministers secretly met the Israeli Prime Minister, David Ben Gurion, in France. Ben Gurion wished to teach the Egyptians a lesson. He wanted to end the border raids from Gaza and to force Egypt to recognise the state of Israel. He also wanted to break the Egyptian **blockade** of the Tiran Straits (see map 8) which prevented ships from reaching the Israeli port of Eilat. France, like Britain and Israel, also wanted to teach Egypt, and especially Nasser, a lesson.

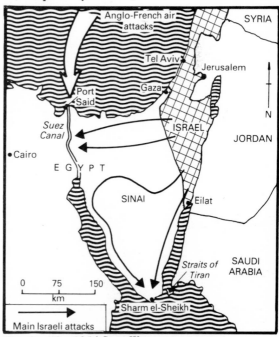

Map 8   The 1956 Suez War.

21

British troops on the banks of the Suez Canal.

War

Five days after this meeting, Israeli forces invaded the Sinai peninsula in Egypt and advanced towards the Suez Canal. The following day, Britain and France ordered Egypt and Israel to cease fighting and withdraw

The Suez Canal blocked by ships, 1956.

16 kilometres from the Canal. If either side refused, Britain and France would use force. The Israelis were still far from the Canal and therefore agreed, but Nasser refused to withdraw from the Canal because it was Egyptian territory. On 31 October, French and British planes bombed Egyptian airfields and destroyed most of the air force. On 5 November British and French troops landed at Port Said and advanced along the Canal. Egypt responded by sinking ships to block the Canal.

Nasser became even more popular amongst the Egyptians and other Arabs. In the United Nations there was massive opposition to Anglo-French action. The Americans were furious that Britain and France had used force and Russia threatened to intervene. On November 6 the UN proclaimed a cease-fire and sent an Emergency Force to the Canal. British and French forces withdrew.

1 Write the heading 'The Second Arab-Israeli War, 1956'.
  (a) Now copy out the following passage filling in the blanks:

    In 1954 . . . became President of Egypt. He wanted to develop Egyptian agriculture and industry. His biggest project was the building of the . . . He also needed to strengthen Egypt's army, especially after the Israeli raid on . . . in February 1955.

    In September he announced that Egypt would buy . . . arms from Czechoslovakia. In July 1956 Britain and the USA decided . . .. Nasser then announced that Egypt would . . . in order to pay for the dam. This made the British and French furious. They held a secret meeting with . . . in France. Five days later, war between Egypt and Israel broke out.

  (b) Copy out the chart below and complete it by writing down the main events of the war.

Date	Events
29 Oct	
30 Oct	
31 Oct	
5 Nov	
6 Nov	

  (c) Suggest at least two headlines that might have appeared in British newspapers on the morning of 31 October or 1 November 1956.
2 Turn to the map you traced in exercise 7, page 18. Using map 8 as a guide, mark on Sinai, Port Said, the Tiran Straits and Eilat.

Leader of the Arab world

Nasser became the hero of the whole Arab world. He had stood up to Britain and France, who had dominated the Middle East for so long, and he had gained complete control of the Canal. He lost territory when the Israelis overran the whole of Sinai, but they were persuaded to withdraw by the Americans in 1957. Besides, Nasser could claim that the Egyptian Army had only been defeated because the Israelis had Anglo-French support.

One of the main effects of the Suez crisis was to make many of the Arab states even more anti-Western and willing to seek Russian aid. The Soviet Union began to supply most of Egypt's weapons and to pay for the building of the Aswan Dam and many other projects. Nasser did not want Egypt to be tied to Russia and he was certainly not a Communist. He wanted Egypt and the other Arab states to be neutral. In 1964 he invited the leaders of the Arab states to a conference in Cairo. Although many of them distrusted each other, they were all united in their opposition to the state of Israel and in their support for the Palestinians.

Exercises
3 In September 1956, a month before the Suez war, the British Prime Minister, Sir Anthony Eden, wrote to the US President:

Source 6
(from *Full Circle* by Sir Anthony Eden, Cassell 1960)

. . . the seizure of the Suez Canal is, we are convinced, the opening gambit [move] in a planned campaign designed by Nasser to expel all Western influence and interests from Arab countries. He believes that if he can get away with this . . . his prestige in Arabia will be so great that he will be able to mount revolutions of young officers in Saudi Arabia, Jordan, Syria and Iraq . . . These new governments will have to place their united oil resources under the control of a united Arabia led by Egypt and under Russian influence. When that moment comes Nasser can deny oil to Western Europe and we here shall all be at his mercy.

  (a) Do you think Eden is expressing facts or opinions? Explain your answer.
  (b) What are Eden's four main fears?
  (c) How do you think Nasser would answer these accusations?

4 Read the following extracts about the consequences of the Suez War.

Source 7
(from *The Elusive Peace*, W. Polk, Croom Helm, 1979)

Israel gained one objective — passage through Egyptian territorial waters in the Straits of Tiran to its port at Eilat on the Gulf of Aqaba. . . .

Curiously, in Western eyes, the Suez War made Nasser a hero. One of its purposes was to destroy him and at the beginning of the fighting few would have given him even odds to survive. However, he did; more, he claimed with some justice a diplomatic victory within a military defeat.

Source 8
(from *Cold War to Detente 1945–80*, Bown and Mooney, Heinemann, 1981)

The Suez incident was a bonus for the Soviet Union and little short of a disaster for the West. . . . it seriously damaged Anglo-French and Western prestige in the Middle East; the leading Arab opponents of continued Western dominance in the area, Egypt and Syria, turned increasingly to the Soviet Union for the arms and aid that they needed, which the West was reluctant to supply. Suez gave the USSR a foothold in the Middle East . . . .

(a) Are these primary or secondary sources? What advantages and disadvantages do such sources have for the historian?
(b) With what justice could Nasser claim 'a diplomatic victory within a military defeat'?
(c) Using these sources and what you have read in the chapter, explain what effect the war had on (i) Soviet and (ii) Anglo-French influence in the Middle East.
(d) 'The Israelis gained little from the war because they had to withdraw from the land they had conquered'. Explain whether you agree or disagree with this statement.

6

The Six-Day War

El-Fatah's raids

At their meeting in Cairo in 1964, leaders of the Arab states decided to set up the Palestine Liberation Organisation (PLO). The aim of this organisation was to win back the land which the Palestinians had lost in 1948–9. In 1965 a **guerrilla** group called **el-Fatah** carried out its first raid on Israel. This group carried out many violent raids into Israel over the next few years. They also planted bombs in Israeli government buildings and mined roads.

The state of Israel had become richer and more modern since the 1956 war. Industries had been built and huge areas of desert irrigated. Israel had also spent vast sums of money on her armed forces to defend herself. This was only possible with huge gifts from abroad. Most of this aid came from the USA. In fact, the US Government and American Jews sent about $1000 million a year to Israel. The US Government felt that Israel was a close, firm friend in a troubled part of the world and they knew that Russia was arming Egypt and Syria.

Syria, Jordan and Lebanon were the three countries where **el-Fatah** had its bases. All three bordered Israel (see map 9 on page 28). Israeli villages were often attacked by **el-Fatah** **guerrillas**. The governments of Lebanon and Jordan tried to restrict PLO activities because they were afraid of Israeli **reprisals**. The Syrians, however, were very keen to support the PLO. They encouraged **el-Fatah's** raids against Israel and supplied men and arms. The only neighbouring state from which Israel was not attacked was Egypt. This was because United Nations troops had been placed on the border between Egypt and Israel after the 1956 war to prevent further clashes. These

UN troops were either in the crowded Gaza Strip, or at Sharm-el-Sheikh guarding the passage of Israeli ships through the Straits of Tiran and the Gulf of Aqaba to Eilat (see map 9 on page 28).

UN troops at Sharm-el-Sheikh, 1967.

In 1966 the Syrians became even more anti-Israeli and accused the Egyptian Government of not supporting them. They said that President Nasser was hiding behind the protection of the UN troops. Nasser was deeply hurt. He wanted his country to remain peaceful, but he also wanted to remain the leader of the Arab world. He knew that the Arabs looked to him to help the Palestinians return to their country. So, in November 1966, he signed a defence agreement with the Syrian Government although he hoped to avoid starting another war with Israel.

25

Tension was not only high in Syria, for a week later a mine exploded on the Israeli–Jordan frontier, killing three Israeli soldiers. The Israelis **retaliated** by attacking the nearest Jordanian village. In early 1967 there were many more raids and **reprisals** across the borders. Israeli villages near the Syrian border were frequently shelled by Syrian guns. In April 1967 the Israeli air force shot down six Syrian MiG fighters after a Syrian attack on Northern Israel. In May, Russia warned her Syrian ally that Israel was preparing to attack.

Crisis in May 1967

On 18 May Nasser asked the UN commander to remove his troops from Egyptian soil. He wanted to prove that Egypt was completely independent. The UN forces could only stay on Egyptian territory as long as Egypt allowed them and the Israelis would not permit the UN troops on their side of the border. The UN troops were withdrawn. The PLO and the leaders of Syria, Jordan and Iraq now challenged Nasser to take control of the Gulf of Aqaba again (see map 9 on page 28). In a speech Nasser proclaimed Egypt's

sovereignty over the Gulf of Aqaba . . . Under no circumstances will we allow the Israeli flag to pass through the Gulf of Aqaba.

The Israelis regarded this as 'an act of aggression' against Israel, and claimed that the USA, France and Britain had 'guaranteed' free passage for all shipping through the Gulf of Aqaba in 1957.

Meanwhile, a war fever was being whipped up in the press and radio in several Arab states. In Jordan, King Hussein wanted to avoid war and remain neutral if fighting broke out. But half the population of Jordan was Palestinian, and newspapers and demonstrations demanded revenge for 1948. At the end of May 1967 King Hussein signed a defence treaty with Egypt. Nasser now made more demands:

The issue now at hand is not the Gulf of Aqaba, the Straits of Tiran, or the withdrawal of the UN forces, but the rights of the Palestine people. It is the

aggression which took place in Palestine in 1948 with the collaboration of Britain and the United States.

He demanded that Israel should allow the Palestinian **refugees** to return to Israel and that Israel should give up the land she had taken in the 1948–9 war (which was more than the UN had offered her). Maybe he thought that Israel would give way and he could win a victory without war.

The Israelis now feared a repeat of 1948. They were surrounded by warlike Arab states. They decided to attack first. Just after dawn on Monday 5 June the Israeli air force took off. They attacked the Arab planes on the ground. Within four hours they had destroyed the air forces of Egypt, Syria and Jordan. The war was to last six days but Israel had virtually won on the first morning. The main facts of the fighting are presented on the table.

Israeli tanks preparing to attack.

Winning the peace

The Israelis had won a brilliant military victory. The Arabs had larger armies but their air forces were destroyed. The Arabs had modern Soviet missiles and other weapons but the Israelis had the most advanced electronic equipment and were highly skilled and well-trained. Above all, the Israelis believed they were fighting for their nation's survival. Now, however, they had to win the peace. They had to decide what to do with all the lands they had seized.

Date	Israel v. Egypt	Israel v. Jordan	Israel v. Syria
Monday 5 June	Israeli planes bombed all 19 Egyptian airfields and wrecked 300 planes. Israeli troops advanced into Gaza Strip and Sinai desert.	The Israelis destroyed the Jordanian airforce. Jordanian troops attacked West Jerusalem.	Israeli planes crippled the Syrian airforce.
Tuesday 6 June	The Israelis raced the Egyptian forces to the Suez Canal. The Israeli airforce destroyed many Egyptian tanks and other vehicles, while Israeli ground forces destroyed or captured the rest.	Heavy fighting for control of Jerusalem and of the West Bank of the River Jordan.	
Wednesday 7 June	The Israelis won complete control of Sinai and accepted the UN call for a cease-fire with Egypt.	The Israelis captured all of Jerusalem. Jordan accepted the UN demand for a cease-fire.	
Thursday 8 June	Egypt accepted the cease-fire call.	Israel won complete control of all the West Bank of the River Jordan.	
Friday 9 June			Israeli troops attacked the Golan Heights.
Saturday 10 June			Israelis seized the Golan Heights. Syria accepted the UN call for a cease-fire.

Main events of the Six-Day War, 1967.

Map 9   Israeli gains in 1967.

Gaza Strip — a narrow piece of land on the coast. It is densely populated with 300 000 inhabitants, mostly Palestinian Arabs. It was from Gaza that many raids were launched against Israel in the 1950s.

Golan Heights — an area of high ground which dominates much of northern Israel and the route to the Syrian capital, Damascus. Between 1948 and 1967 the Syrians held the Heights, and before the war Syrian troops shelled Israeli settlements from these hills. Most of the 100 000 Syrian inhabitants fled during the fighting.

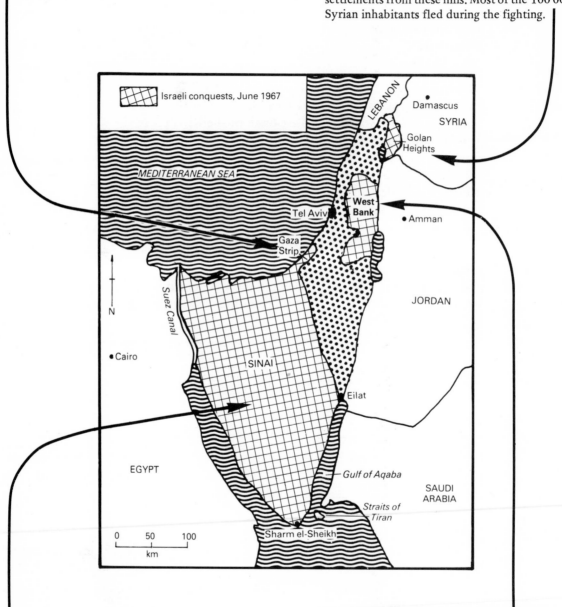

Sinai — a large area of Egyptian territory. It is mostly desert. Very few people live here. On the western side is the Suez Canal and to the south-east is the Gulf of Aqaba.

West Bank of River Jordan — this area had been part of the Arab state of Jordan since the 1948–9 war; 750 000 people, mostly Palestinian Arabs, lived here (the population of Israel is about 2.5 million). Parts of the West Bank are very fertile, especially in the river valley.

Exercises

1 It is mid-June 1967. You are an adviser to the Israeli government. The Prime Minister is seeking your opinion on the future of the lands which the army has occupied since the recent war. Study map 9 and read the information about each of the occupied lands which is given at the sides. Decide what policy you recommend for each area. There are three main policies to be considered:

Annexation — Making the land part of the state of Israel and giving the people full rights as Israeli citizens.

Military Occupation — Keeping troops in the area to maintain law and order, treating the inhabitants as foreigners.

Negotiation — Trying to make a deal with your Arab enemies with a view to giving back their land.

When deciding your policy you should consider:

* The peace and security of the Israeli state and people.
* The cost and difficulty of enforcing the policy.
* The reactions of the inhabitants, the US government, the Arab states and other powers.

You might also consider other factors. Decide what policy you would recommend for each area in turn. Using the box below, you can tick the policy you think is the most suitable but you must also prepare a report in which you explain the reasons for your decision.

	OCCUPIED LANDS			
Policies	Golan Heights	West Bank	Gaza Strip	Sinai
Annexation				
Military Occupation				
Negotiation				

After the war

The Israelis argued with each other about the occupied lands (and they still do today) but most of them agreed that Jews must dominate them. In fact, the Israeli Government decided on military occupation of the conquered lands. They also ordered the army to confiscate Arab land and build Jewish settlements in order to make the areas more secure.

On one point, in particular, the Israelis were united. They had taken control of the remaining part of Jerusalem, the Old City, for the first time in nearly 2000 years. They were determined to hold on to it. As the Israeli Defence Minister, General Dayan, said on the radio:

We have unified Jerusalem, the divided capital of Israel. We have returned to the holiest of our Holy places, never to part from it again.

Israeli troops enter the Old City of Jerusalem (General Dayan is in the centre).

29

Israel's borders were secure. There was a buffer zone between her land and each of her three main enemies (see map 9). Villages in the north were safe from Syrian artillery now that the Israelis controlled the Golan Heights. Military fortifications were built on the banks of the River Jordan and the Suez Canal, while the Sinai Desert formed a huge buffer between Israel and the Egyptian army.

The Arabs felt more hostile than ever. They blamed their defeat on the USA, Britain and other European powers, whom they accused of helping Israel in the war. At a meeting in August 1967 Arab leaders declared that their main principles were:

No peace with Israel, no recognition of Israel, no negotiation with it, and insistence on the rights of the Palestinian people in their own country.

The three main oil-producing Arab states of Saudi Arabia, Kuwait and Libya agreed to pay £135 million annually to Egypt and Jordan, the two states which had suffered most in the war. The Soviet Union also decided to replace the weapons which its allies had lost in the war.

In November 1967 the United Nations called for 'the withdrawal of Israeli armed forces from territories occupied in the recent conflict', and respect for the right of all Middle East states to 'live in peace within secure and recognised boundaries'. However, the Israelis would not withdraw and the Arabs would not recognise the state of Israel.

In 1968 fighting between Israel and Egypt broke out again. The Egyptians wished to clear the Suez Canal of sunken ships. The Israelis would only agree to this if their ships were allowed through the Canal. Over the next two years there were many clashes across the Canal. Both sides lost many men and weapons. By 1970 both sides were tiring. Nasser had not received the support he hoped for from the other Arab states. He appeared willing to recognize Israel. Then, in September 1970, he died. He had played an important part in world affairs for nearly 20 years.

Exercises

2 In List A are the beginnings of seven sentences. Choose the correct ending for each sentence from List B. Make the heading 'The Six-Day War'. Then write down the sentences in the correct order.

List A	List B
In May 1967	Israeli planes wiped out the Arab air forces.
In 1966 and early 1967	Israel controlled all of the original state of Palestine.
On 7 June 1967	Nasser ordered the UN troops to leave Egypt and closed the Gulf of Aqaba to Israeli ships.
After four days of war	the Israelis shot down six Syrian planes.
On a reprisal raid in April 1967	the Israelis had won a decisive victory over Egypt, Jordan and Syria.
On 5 June 1967	Israeli forces won complete control of Sinai.
On 10 June 1967	el-Fatah made many raids into Israel.

3 Read the following statements. Write down the ones which explain why Israel won the Six-Day War.
   A The Arabs were surprised by the Israeli attack.
   B The Arab air forces were destroyed on the first day.
   C The Arabs had to rely on old out-of-date weapons.
   D The Israelis were well-equipped and highly trained.
   E The Israelis had larger armies than the Arabs.
   F The Israeli forces were supported by US troops.
   G The Israelis believed they were fighting to save their nation.
4 In what ways were the geographical boundaries of Israel easier to defend after the 1967 war?

7
Terrorism

WEATHER:
Sunny spells.
Lighting-up time:
8.8 p.m.
Details—Back Page.   46,082

Evening Standard

CITY PRICES

London: Tuesday September 5 1972   5   3p

Arab terrorists gun down Israelis in Munich village —hold 13 as hostages

POLICE POUR INTO THE OLYMPIC VILLAGE AFTER THE ATTACK.

MURDER AT THE OLYMPICS

Standard Foreign News Desk

ARAB COMMANDOS armed with sub-machine guns invaded the Olympic Village in Munich today killed two

kong team, housed adjacent to the Israeli quarters, said he was awakened by noises between 4 a.m. and 5 a.m.
He said: " I saw a man carrying what looked like a sub-machine gun walking up and down the stairs. Then I heard shots. German security police came on the scene. I saw one man being carried away on a stretcher and presumed he had been shot dead."

On 5 September 1972 Palestinian **guerrillas** attacked the Israeli athletes who were competing in the Olympic Games in Germany. They killed two athletes on the spot and then demanded the release of 200 Palestinians in prison in Israel. When German police attempted a rescue, the Palestinians killed nine more athletes. The Palestinians got the massive publicity they wanted for their cause but not the release of their comrades. A few days later the Israelis took their revenge and killed over 200 Palestinian **refugees** in Syria and Lebanon.

This was not the first time that Arabs or Israelis had carried out what we call terrorist acts. For example, in 1948, Jewish terrorists attacked and killed the inhabitants of the village of Deir Yassin (see Chapter 4). Then in the 1950s Palestinian **guerrillas** carried out many raids against Israeli villages. But after the Six Day War, the terrorism spread to Europe and our newspapers reported it in full. To understand the reasons for the spread of terrorism we must look back to see what happened to the Palestinians after 1948.

The Palestinian refugees

During the fighting in 1948—9 about 700 000 Arabs fled from their homes in Palestine. As you can see on map 10, most of them went to the West Bank or to the Gaza Strip. Others went to Syria, Jordan and Lebanon. After the war the United Nations Organisation set up camps for the **refugees** and provided food, clothing, shelter and education. Some Palestinians were lucky enough to get jobs in their new countries and a small number became very wealthy, but most of them remained poor, uneducated and unemployed. Crowded together in the camps, they became frustrated and bitter and hoped to return to Palestine one day.

The Palestinians were scattered over many lands. The Palestine Liberation Organisation aimed to unite them all in the struggle to win back their land. Egypt, Syria and Jordan

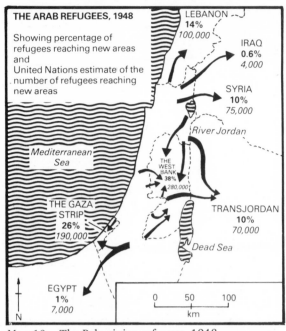

THE ARAB REFUGEES, 1948

Showing percentage of refugees reaching new areas and United Nations estimate of the number of refugees reaching new areas

LEBANON
14%
100,000

IRAQ
0.6%
4,000

SYRIA
10%
75,000

River Jordan

Mediterranean Sea

THE WEST BANK
38%
280,000

TRANSJORDAN
10%
70,000

THE GAZA STRIP
26%
190,000

Dead Sea

EGYPT
1%
7,000

N

0   50   100
km

Map 10   The Palestinian refugees, 1948.

A Palestinian refugee camp.

provided vital support for the PLO, but these three countries were weakened by their heavy losses in the Six Day War of 1967. They became more concerned about the lands they had lost than about the Palestinian **refugees**. Many Palestinians were now convinced that they would have to fight for their homeland on their own. This was even more urgent now that all the original state of Palestine, including the West Bank and Gaza Strip, was under Israeli rule. They looked for arms and money in Europe and the Soviet Union as well as in the Arab countries. The PLO recruited more volunteers in the **refugee** camps.

In 1968, at Karameh in Jordan, PLO forces (with Jordanian troops) successfully resisted an Israeli **reprisal** raid. Several Israeli tanks and planes were destroyed and this inspired thousands of Palestinians to join the Palestinian armed forces. The strongest Palestinian group was **el-Fatah** and in 1968 its leader, Yasser Arafat, became chairman of the PLO.

Hijacks and hostages

Arafat and most of the PLO leaders wanted to limit the raids and bombings to Israeli territory because their military aim was strictly war on Israel. However, some **extremist** Palestinian groups caused a division inside the PLO by making attacks in other parts of the world. They were impatient and were not prepared to wait ten or twenty years. These Palestinians realised that raids into Israel achieved little.

In December 1968 two Palestinians hijacked an Israeli passenger plane at Athens airport, killing one man. The Israelis **retaliated** by destroying 13 aircraft in an attack on Beirut Airport in Lebanon which is where the two Palestinian hijackers had come from. In the following years there were many hijackings, kidnappings and bombings in Europe and elsewhere. At first the targets were Israeli planes, embassies and offices, but some targets had very little to do with Israel at all. The Israelis usually responded by bombing Palestinian bases in Lebanon and Syria. Often these bases were near **refugee** camps so that hundreds of innocent Palestinians died. These Israeli **reprisals** received far less publicity in the Western press than the Palestinian attacks.

Acts of terrorism made the Palestinians unpopular in the West where people were shocked by such brutal deeds. But many began to think more about the Palestinian problem. They realised that the Palestinian people were the helpless victims of war. They read about the crowded, unhealthy camps in which hundreds of thousands of refugees had lived for 20 years. One Palestinian leader said:

Source 9

When we hijack a plane it has more effect than if we killed a hundred Israelis in battle. For decades world public opinion has been neither for nor against the Palestinians. It simply ignored us. At least the world is talking about us now.

Yet the violence continued and sometimes led Arab to fight Arab. In Jordan, King Hussein still feared Israeli **reprisals** and he ordered the Palestinians to obey him and his army. Then in September 1970 four aircraft were hijacked by Palestinian **extremists** and three of them (belonging to British Airways, Swissair and TWA) were taken to a Palestinian base in Jordan. This made King Hussein fear foreign intervention and he was forced to act. He ordered his army to take control of the Palestinian bases. The Palestinians resisted and in the next ten days nearly 10 000 of them were killed. The PLO offices were shut down and their newspapers banned. The remaining **guerrillas** went to Syria and Lebanon.

Palestinian **extremists** later got their revenge by murdering the Jordanian Prime Minister while he was in Egypt. These were members of a group called Black September, named after the month in which the Palestinian bases in Jordan were wiped out. Soon they began sending letter bombs to Israeli embassies in Europe, then in September 1972 they killed the Israeli athletes at the Olympic Games (see page 31).

These acts of terrorism were carried out to force foreign governments to do something about the Palestinian problem. The **extremists** also hoped to prevent any Arab-Israeli treaty between Jordan or Egypt and Israel, because they believed that such a treaty would ignore the Palestinians.

The British Airways plane which was hijacked by Palestinians is blown up at an airfield in Jordan.

Exercises

In this exercise you will be examining different views of the Palestinians and considering the methods they have used to publicise their cause.

Source 10
(Palestinian National Charter, July 1968)

Palestine is the homeland of the Palestinian Arab people; it is an indivisible part of the Arab homeland, and the Palestinian people are an integral part of the Arab nation .... The Palestinians are those Arab nationals who, until 1947, normally resided in Palestine regardless of whether they were evicted from it or have stayed there. Anyone born, after that date, of a Palestinian father − whether inside Palestine or outside it − is also a Palestinian .... The Jews who had normally resided in Palestine until the beginning of the Zionist invasion will be considered Palestinians.

Source 11
(Israeli Prime Minister, Golda Meir, 1969, quoted in *The Palestinian Liberation Organisation*, Helena Cobban, Cambridge)

It was not as though there was a Palestinian people ... and we came and threw them out and took their country away from them. They did not exist.

Source 12
(Sami el-Karami, quoted in *Dispossessed: Ordeal of the Palestinians*, David Gilmour, Sphere)

The non-violent methods are very beautiful and very easy, and we wish we could win with these methods. Our people do not carry machine-guns and bombs because they enjoy killing. It is for us the last resort. For twenty-two years we waited for the United Nations and the United States, for liberty, for freedom and democracy. There was no result. So this is our last resort.

Source 13
(letter from a Palestinian student in Beirut to his parents, 1968)

For twenty years our people have been waiting for a just solution to the Palestinian problem. All that we got was charity and humiliation while others continue to live in our homes. I refuse to remain a refugee. I have decided to join the freedom fighters and I ask for your blessings.

1 List three groups of people who, according to Source 10, are to be considered Palestinians.
2 How can the author of Source 11 claim that Palestinians 'did not exist'? Why would she wish to make this claim?
3 According to the authors of Sources 9 (on page 33), 12 and 13, why have the Palestinians used violent methods?
4 In Source 13, the student calls himself a 'freedom fighter'. Why does he use this term rather than 'terrorist'?
5 Palestinian terrorist attacks received far more publicity than Israeli **reprisals** although the latter usually led to more deaths. How would you explain this?
6 What doubts would an historian of the Palestinian problem have about using the following sources as evidence:
   (a) official statements of organisations and leaders (as in Sources 10 and 11)?
   (b) the views of 'terrorists' (as in sources 9, 12 and 13)?
7 Why, none the less, might the historian find such sources valuable?

8
Oil and War

President Sadat

There had been much bloodshed and terrible suffering on both the Arab and Israeli sides since the 1940s, yet a peace settlement was still far off. In 1970 Anwar Sadat took over from Nasser as President of Egypt. Like Nasser, he was an army officer. He promised his people that the year 1971 'would not end without the conflict with Israel having been settled'.

President Sadat of Egypt.

There was still great tension on the Suez Canal. Neither side could use the Canal although both sides wanted to, and it seemed that fighting could flare up at any time. Egypt had to keep nearly a million men ready to fight and this was very expensive. She needed peace in order to clear the Suez Canal and rebuild her cities. But she also wanted to win back the Sinai, the land east of the Suez Canal which she had lost in 1967.

Sadat was prepared to recognise the state of Israel in order to regain the lost land. However, the Israelis were unwilling to discuss it and Sadat knew he could not defeat Israel in war. He therefore tried to get help from the USA to force Israel to give way. The USA was very friendly with Israel, but Sadat knew the US Government wanted peace and friendship with the Arab states in the Middle East. As an Arab, Sadat hoped he could persuade the US Government to use its influence with the Israelis. He sacked the members of his government who were anti-American. The USA, however, was too busy with the war in Vietnam. Besides, the 6 million Jews in America would not allow the US Government to bully the Israelis. So the year 1971 ended, as it had begun, with 'no peace, no war'.

Sadat then tried to obtain support from the Russians but, in return for supplying arms for Egypt, they wanted more control in Egyptian affairs. The Egyptian Government could not stand any more Russian interference and so, in 1972, Sadat expelled all 15 000 Russian advisers who had been training Egypt's armed forces. This still made little difference to America's attitude. However, Sadat now had strong financial support from the oil-rich state of Saudi Arabia. Also, the new Syrian leader, President Assad, became a close ally. Both men realised they would never regain the lands they had lost in 1967 unless they acted soon. Secretly, the Egyptian and Syrian leaders prepared for war. Meanwhile, in August 1973, the Israeli Government decided to start building more towns in the occupied land. In the following month, in a speech in Cairo, President Sadat said:

Source 14

The United States is still under **Zionist** pressure and is wearing **Zionist** spectacles. The United States will have to take off those spectacles before they talk to us . . . We have had enough talk. We know our goal and we are determined to attain it.

Very few people took him seriously. They had heard it all before. So had the Israelis. They had a low opinion of the Arab armies anyway.

The Yom Kippur War, 1973

On October 6 Egypt and Syria attacked. It was the day of the Jewish holiday of **Yom Kippur**. This meant that many soldiers were on leave and Israeli radio was closed down. The Israelis were caught completely by surprise. The Egyptians crossed the Suez Canal and took back part of Sinai from the Israelis.

Tanks wrecked in the Yom Kippur War.

36

At the same time, 500 Syrian tanks over-whelmed Israeli forces on the Golan Heights. The Israeli air force retaliated but discovered that the Arabs had very effective Soviet missiles. It took the Israeli army three days to become fully **mobilised**. Then, by October 12, they had pushed the Syrians back, and on October 15 they thrust across the Suez Canal and cut off the Egyptian third army (see map 11).

Two days later the Arabs produced an unexpected weapon — oil. The West received much of its oil from the Middle East. The Arab oil-producing states decided to reduce oil production until the Israelis withdrew from the lands they had occupied in 1967. The richest oil state, Saudi Arabia, went further. It banned all oil exports to the USA and Netherlands, the two countries which were accused of helping Israel the most. The West was shocked.

The superpowers step in

The USA and USSR were deeply involved in the **Yom Kippur** War. The Russians sent arms to Egypt and Syria and the USA sent them to the Israelis. When the Israelis crossed the Suez Canal both superpowers stepped in. Russia advised Egypt to accept a cease-fire while she held part of Sinai. The US Government was

worried by the Arab oil weapon. It also hoped to keep its ally away from Cairo and Damascus for fear that Russian troops might be brought in. Both superpowers were keen to be on good terms with each other. American and Russian leaders met and together demanded a cease-fire which the United Nations supported. The fighting ended on 24 October. A few days later UN troops were sent to Egypt to preserve the cease-fire.

The Arabs gain new confidence

The **Yom Kippur** War was, in the end, a military victory for the Israelis. Yet again they had proved that their weapons, their training and their tactics were superior. But it was a political victory for the Arabs. They had completely surprised the Israelis and the rest of the world with their attack. They had proved that the Arab soldiers could fight with courage and determination. Their leaders had shown skill. Above all, they had acted

Reduced oil production meant petrol shortages in Britain and other countries in the West.

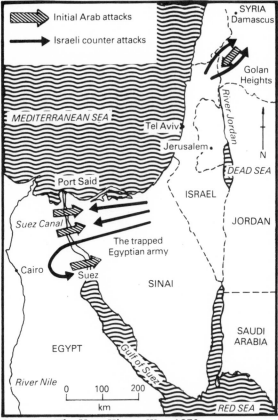

Map 11   The Yom Kippur War, 1973.

together, especially in the use of the oil weapon. As a result the rest of the world showed far more respect for the Arabs.

One man, in particular, emerged from the war as a hero. Anwar Sadat had achieved exactly what he set out to do. First he had broken the stalemate that existed before the war. Secondly, he had forced a change in US policy. America was to become far more friendly with the Arab states. A few years later the American Government was to play an important part in bringing about peace between Egypt and Israel.

Exercises

1 Read Source 14 on page 36. President Sadat made this speech a week before the war broke out.
    (a) What does he mean when he accuses the USA of wearing '**Zionist** spectacles'?
    (b) Do you think it is a fair accusation? Give reasons.
    (c) What had he already done to encourage the Americans 'to take off those spectacles'?
    (d) What finally made the United States 'take off those spectacles' and talk to the Egyptians'?

2 (a) What were the main reasons for the war of Yom Kippur of 1973? In what ways were these reasons the same as those for the earlier wars (1948, 1956 and 1967) and in what ways were they different?
    (b) Did the Arab countries use any new tactics or weapons in this war and, if so, how effective were they?
    (c) Compare the outcome of the 1973 war with the earlier wars — who won and who lost, and in what ways?

9
Peace and the Palestinians

After the Yom Kippur War, the US Government worked hard to bring peace to the Middle East. Henry Kissinger, the US Secretary of State for Foreign Affairs, flew many times between Egypt, Israel and Syria. He managed to persuade both the Israelis and Egyptians to draw back their forces on the Suez Canal in January 1974. In March, Saudi Arabia started selling oil to the USA again. In May, Syria and Israel agreed to separate their forces on the Golan Heights. The following year, the Suez Canal was re-opened and the Israeli and Egyptian forces drew back on the Sinai front also. An international force kept the two sides apart.

However, the Arab states were still determined to win back the lands they had lost in 1967. They seemed willing to recognise the state of Israel although they did not admit this in public. Even Yasser Arafat and some of the PLO leaders sounded more moderate. They said that they were ready to consider a 'mini-state' for the Palestinians — consisting of the West Bank and Gaza where the majority of the inhabitants were Palestinian. In other words, the PLO **moderates** were no longer determined to remove the state of Israel. They realised the value of foreign political support and set up PLO offices in many countries. PLO officials set out to win the support of foreign governments. At the end of 1974 Yasser Arafat was invited to speak at the United Nations. He told his audience that the roots of the Palestine question

do not stem from any conflict between two religions or two nationalisms. Neither is it a border conflict between two neighbouring states. It is the cause of people deprived of its homeland, dispersed and uprooted, and living mostly in exile and in **refugee** camps.

Palestinians on the West Bank.

Many of his listeners were sympathetic. Some world leaders were beginning to admit that the Palestinians deserved a homeland. They also realised that if the Palestinians could be granted a homeland, then permanent peace in the Middle East was possible. Yasser Arafat ended his speech to the UN with the words:

Today I have come bearing an olive branch and a freedom fighter's gun. Do not let the olive branch fall from my hand.

Arafat speaking to the UN.

wanted permanent peace for his own country. Four wars against Israel had cost many lives and much money. Egypt needed a lasting peace to recover. In 1977 he announced that he was willing to go to Israel and discuss peace. This was a bold move; for 30 years Arab leaders had refused even to accept Israel's existence..

Ten days later Sadat became the first Arab leader to go to Israel. He spoke to the Israeli parliament:

We used to reject you, and we had our reasons and grievances . . . But I say to you today and I say to the whole world that we accept that we should live with you in lasting and just peace.

The following month the Israeli Prime Minister, Menachem Begin, went to Egypt and peace talks were started. When they slowed down in 1978, US President Carter invited the Egyptian and Israeli leaders to Camp David in America. For 13 days the three men discussed a peace settlement in secret. Two agreements were reached and the hopes they expressed are outlined in the box opposite.

However, Yasser Arafat had many enemies. The Israelis were furious with the United Nations for inviting Arafat to speak. They said the PLO was a 'murder organisation'. They refused to discuss the idea of a separate Palestinian state, however small it might be. They feared that the Palestinians aimed to take back the country that was now Israel, and would not be content with a small state next door to Israel.

The PLO itself was divided. Some **extremists** still insisted that Israel should be destroyed and taken over by Palestinians. They rejected the idea of a Palestinian 'mini-state' and did not want any Arab government to recognise the state of Israel. In the mid-1970s they launched terrorist attacks both inside Israel and in other parts of the world. The Israelis retaliated by bombing the Palestinian bases and **refugee** camps in Lebanon.

Camp David

President Sadat of Egypt hoped to solve the Palestinian question. However, above all, he

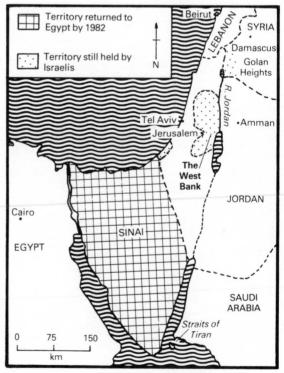

Map 12   Israel and her Arab neighbours, 1978.

1 A Framework for Peace in the Middle East; the main points are:
* Palestinians on the West Bank and Gaza will elect a council to govern themselves for five years.
* Israeli troops will be gradually withdrawn from these two areas (although a small security force will remain).
* Israel, Egypt and Jordan and Palestinian representatives will decide how the West Bank and Gaza should be ruled at the end of five years.
* It is hoped that Israel will make peace treaties with all her Arab neighbours.

2 A framework for an Egypt–Israel Peace Treaty:
* Egypt will regain all of Sinai within three years.
* Israeli forces will withdraw from Sinai.
* Israeli shipping will have free passage through the Suez Canal and the Straits of Tiran.

Six months later, in March 1979, the Egyptian and Israeli leaders signed a peace treaty. The Israelis agreed to withdraw from Sinai and the Egyptians agreed to allow Israeli ships to pass through the Suez Canal and Straits of Tiran. Both sides finally agreed to recognise 'each other's right to live in peace within their secure and recognised boundaries'.

South Lebanon is 'Fatahland'

Although the USA had tried to bring peace to the Middle East at Camp David, the fighting continued after 1978. Lebanon was the next major flashpoint because the PLO armed forces had concentrated there after they were expelled from Jordan in 1970 (see page 33). They took over most of the south of Lebanon (some called it Fatahland) and frequently bombed villages in northern Israel. In 1978 a PLO suicide squad went further south and attacked a bus near Tel Aviv, killing 37 passengers. Three days later Israeli armed forces invaded Lebanon. They seized the south of the country but the PLO forces melted away. The Israelis withdrew under UN and American influence and UN troops were

Begin and Sadat shake hands at Camp David while Carter looks on.

PLO forces are trained at a Palestinian camp.

Israeli tanks advance into Lebanon, June 1982.

sent to keep the peace on the Lebanese-Israeli border.

Four years later, in 1982, after a Palestinian attempt to murder the Israeli ambassador in London, the Israelis again invaded Lebanon to drive out the Palestinian forces. This time they were more successful although thousands of Palestinian and Lebanese civilians were killed in the process. The Israelis advanced north, surrounded the Lebanese capital, Beirut, and bombarded it heavily. After several weeks Yasser Arafat was forced to move his headquarters out of Lebanon to **Tunisia**. Thousands of PLO **guerrillas** were sent to other Arab states.

Although their new bases were more scattered than ever before, the PLO forces were still determined to continue the struggle for Palestine. The **refugees** in the camps regarded the PLO as their leaders. They prayed for The Return and their children took this oath at school:

Palestine is our country
Our aim is to return
Death does not frighten us,
Palestine is ours,
We shall never forget her
Another homeland we shall never accept!
Our Palestine, witness, O God and History
We promise to shed our blood for you!

Other Palestinians, like those living on the West Bank and in Gaza also looked to the PLO for leadership. In the future much will depend on the relations between the Israelis and the million Palestinians living in these occupied territories. In the 1970s and early 1980s the West Bank and Gaza were still ruled by the Israeli army although they were not part of the state of Israel. The Israelis claimed that even if the Palestinians in these areas were given self-government, these lands would still be Jewish, as this is stated in the Bible. The Israeli army continued to confiscate land and build more Jewish settlements.

Source 15 (from *Dispossessed: Ordeal of the Palestinians*, David Gilmour, Sphere)

A site is chosen, the Israeli army moves in, barbed wire is erected and the flag is flown from the nearest piece of high ground. Over the following months concrete buildings are put up and the land is levelled by army bulldozers. Finally the planting begins and greenhouses are erected.

By 1986 there were about 80 000 Jews living in settlements in Jerusalem and another 20 000 in other parts of the West Bank and in Gaza.

Crisis in Lebanon

Until the 1970s Lebanon was fairly stable and Beirut, the capital, was one of the richest cities in the Middle East. However, many Lebanese people were killed in clashes between the PLO and the Israelis in the south. In 1975 the Lebanese government ordered its army to regain control of the south. The Palestinians resisted and were helped by Lebanese Muslims. Most of the Lebanese army were Christians and soon there was a civil war between Christians and Muslims in Lebanon.

In 1976, Syrian forces entered Lebanon to end the fighting and restore order. However, the Palestinians continued to attack Israeli villages and this led to the Israeli invasions in 1978 and 1982. The Israelis remained in South Lebanon after 1982 and the Syrians remained in the east of the country. Amin Gemayel, a Christian, became President of Lebanon in 1982, but many Muslims and Druze (a religious group who are similar to the Muslims) opposed his government. A multinational force of American, French, Italian and British troops tried to preserve peace.

Many Lebanese groups hated the foreign troops, especially the Americans, in their country. In October 1983 a suicide truck bomb drove into the US military headquarters in Beirut and killed 241 American soldiers. Soon after, the Americans left. In 1985 the Israelis realised they had failed to control Lebanon and they began to withdraw their troops.

Into the future

Unless the Palestinians are granted a land of their own there is unlikely to be permanent peace in the Middle East. The West Bank and Gaza are the most obvious areas for such a homeland — most of the inhabitants are Palestinian and they are the only areas of the original Palestine not a part of Israel. The Israelis will have to withdraw from their new Jewish settlements and the Palestinians will have to accept the state of Israel. Both sides will have to learn to be neighbours. Will the Israelis ever be able to forget their fears of Palestinian attacks? Will the Palestinians ever be able to bury their hopes of winning back all of Palestine?

Yasser Arafat and other **moderate** Palestinian leaders in the early 1980s were ready to accept a small Palestinian state. They spent much time trying to win over the world's leaders to their cause. The majority of the Palestinians in the occupied lands and the refugee camps did not want a long war with Israel and supported Arafat's policy. But the PLO was more divided than ever and some of its leaders wanted to keep up the armed struggle and destroy Israel.

Palestinian **extremist** groups continued to carry out attacks on Israelis abroad. After one such attack in 1985, the Israelis bombed the PLO headquarters in Tunisia. The Libyan leader, Colonel Gaddafi, began to help Palestinian terrorists. He encouraged them in their attacks on Israelis and Americans. In 1986, the USA decided to hit back. American planes bombed Libyan military bases and even

A traditional Arab home is overshadowed by a new Jewish settlement on the West Bank.

some civilian buildings in a huge night-time raid.

The main obstacle to peace between Israel and the Arabs remained — the Palestinian problem. Only the USA could persuade the Israelis to agree to an independent Palestinian state. Yet the Americans did little. King Hussein of Jordan tried to bring Israelis and Palestinians together but Palestinian **extremists** wrecked his plans by stepping up their bomb attacks in Europe and the Middle East. In the mid 1980s, the spirit of Camp David seemed a long way off.

Exercises

1 Write each of the following dates down the left-hand side of a page, leaving three or four lines between each date: 1974, 1977, 1978, 1979, 1982.
Beside each date, write what happened in that year and why it was important. If you can think of more than one event in any year, choose the one which you think is the most important.

2 (a) What do you think Yasser Arafat meant when he said to the UN 'Today I have come bearing an olive branch and a freedom fighter's gun. Do not let the olive branch fall from my hand'?

(b) At the Camp David talks in 1978 the Israeli Prime Minister was very reluctant to discuss the Palestinian question. What reasons can you suggest for this?

3 Study the following article from the *Daily Mail* of Tuesday, 27 March, 1979:

Source 16

Against a theatrical backdrop designed to give the best possible political advantage to President Carter, the Egyptian President and the Israeli Prime Minister yesterday signed their names to the long-sought peace treaty, thereby formally ending three decades of hostility, non-recognition and war.

Menachem Begin of Israel and Anwar Sadat of Egypt penned their signatures to the English, Arabic and Hebrew versions of the document.

Relief

Officials had worked right through the morning, making final amendments to the text — lending an atmosphere of tension that heightened everyone's evident relief, once the leaders' ink was drying on the paper.

Outside, demonstrators did their best to spoil the White House ceremonial, warning Sadat with placards and shouts that 'The Shah is gone, you'll be next.'

And already the many groups who would wreck the treaty were murmuring in the wings.

Yasser Arafat, speaking in Beirut, warned Carter and Begin that the Palestine Liberation Organisation 'would cut off your hands' for participating in the 'treachery' and the 'conspiracy' of the new agreement. The Egyptian leader was openly threatened with assassination.

In Tehran Arab students smashed their way into the Egyptian Embassy chanting 'death to Sadat'. Thousands of Iranians shouted their support to the PLO.

Israelis marked the signing of the treaty by prayer and thanksgiving, followed by popular celebrations.

But hundreds of thousands of Arabs in the Israeli-occupied areas staged a general strike in protest, and declared a day of mourning.

(a) Which groups of people, according to the author, were opposed to the peace treaty? How did each group express its disapproval?

(b) Why do you think Yasser Arafat regarded the treaty as 'treachery' and 'conspiracy'?

(c) Shouts of 'Death to Sadat' could be heard in many Arab countries in 1979. Two years later the Egyptian President was assassinated by some of his own soldiers. Does this prove that he was killed *because* he signed the peace treaty? Was it inevitable that he would be killed?

4 In Exercise 8 of Chapter 3 you read about a fictional Palestinian Arab farmer called Hassan and his wife Fatima and a fictional Jewish immigrant called Saul and his wife Lotte. The year is now 1986. Both these men and their wives have died but their children are all alive. Hassan's family moved to Jaffa in 1939 then fled to Syria

in 1948. Hassan and Fatima have left three sons and a daughter. They are:
* Mahmoud — a carpenter in a **refugee** camp in Syria. He has spent most of his life in the camp and is married with two children.
* Ali — an active member of the PLO who spends most of his time either in Syria or Lebanon.
* Mansur — lives and works with his uncle's family on the West Bank.
* Fatima — has married a Syrian and lives with her husband and four children in Damascus.

Saul and Lotte worked on a prosperous **kibbutz** in Northern Israel and have left two children, both of whom are Israeli citizens. They are:
* David — an Israeli army captain who returns to the **kibbutz** when he is on leave.
* Rachel — who is married and lives with her family in a Jewish settlement near Jerusalem on the West Bank.

Assume the part of one of these characters and answer the following questions asked by a Western journalist.

(a) Why do you think Yasser Arafat was asked to speak at the United Nations?
(b) What is your opinion of the Camp David agreements?
(c) For what reasons are the Israelis building Jewish settlements on the West Bank?
(d) What is required for a peaceful solution of the Palestine question?
(e) What would your character think of the comments/suggestions made on pages 44–45 under the heading 'Into the future'?
(f) Which of these six characters would be defined as 'Palestinian' according to the Palestinian National Charter (see page 34)?

5 Read the following newspaper extracts.

Source 17
(*The Times*, April 1983)

The King (Hussein of Jordan) is desperately worried that the Israelis will soon have so many Jewish housing complexes on the occupied West Bank that thousands of Palestinians will be squeezed out into Jordan, upsetting the dubious balance of power that already exists.

The King and his Cabinet suspect that Israel intends to permit a Palestinian state to be set up, though in Jordan, not on the West Bank . . . .

Source 18
(*The Sunday Times*, April 1983)

In a hotel in Portugal, a leading PLO moderate, Dr Issam Sartawi, who believed in a dialogue between Israel and the Palestinians, was shot dead . . . . His killer was a brother Palestinian, a member of an extremist splinter group . . . .

(a) What according to Source 17 is King Hussein's great fear? What does he suspect the Israelis of? What motive might the Israelis have for such a plan?
(b) Read page 33 again and explain what happened when thousands of Palestinians were 'squeezed out into Jordan' after 1967.
(c) In Source 18, who was Dr Sartawi? Does the writer explain why he was killed? If so, is his explanation a fact or an opinion? Explain your answer.
(d) What are the advantages and disadvantages of newspaper reports for the historian?

Bibliography

The two best known textbooks on the Middle East are the School Council's *Arab–Israeli Conflict* (Holmes McDougall) and Geoffrey Regan's *Israel and the Arabs* (Cambridge). For a detailed account, read *Israel and the Arabs* by M. Rodinson (Pelican). Chapters 7–14 of *The Arabs* by P. Mansfield are also recommended. M. Gilbert's *The Arab–Israeli Conflict: Its History in Maps* (Weidenfeld & Nicolson) is excellent and contains some explanation of events as well as superb maps. *A Soldier's Diary* by Y. Dayan (Penguin) records a young woman's experiences in the 1967 war. There are several radio and T.V. programmes such as *Israel and the Arab States* in the BBC Twentieth Century History series.

Glossary

alliance	friendship between two or more countries, usually during war
anti-Semitism	actions or feelings of hatred against the Jews
blockade	the blocking of a place by troops or ships to prevent goods reaching it
diaspora	Jews living in many different parts of the world apart from Israel
el-Fatah	a Palestinian organisation whose main aim was to carry out raids against Israel in the struggle to regain Palestine
extremist	a person who has very strong opinions or aims which he or she refuses to change in any circumstances
fedayeen	men trained to carry out raids (literally, those who sacrifice themselves)
guerrilla	a soldier who avoids fighting in open battle when possible; he prefers to use tactics like ambushes and hit-and-run raids
Haganah	a Jewish defence force set up in the 1920s
High Commissioner	British Ambassador representing the British Government
Holocaust	mass murder of the Jews in the Second World War
immigration	the arrival of people to settle in a new country
impartial	being fair, not favouring one side more than another
Irgun	small, secret Jewish organisation fighting for Jewish independence which used terrorist tactics against the British and the Arabs
Kibbutzim	settlements in Israel where people live and work together, farming the land and selling its produce; the children are brought up together rather than in family groups
mandate	power given to a country to look after another country
mobilised	to be fully organised to fight a war
moderate	a person who can accept other people's points of view
nationalise	the government taking over ownership of a company, industry or a piece of land
partition	division into two or more parts
persecute	treat badly and repeatedly harm someone
refugees	people forced to leave their home by war or natural disaster
reprisal	an action against an enemy to stop him from doing something again
repudiate	refuse to accept something or have anything to do with it
retaliate	hit back
synagogue	a building where Jews worship
Yom Kippur	an important Jewish religious day of fasting and annual Jewish holiday
Zionist	one who believes that the Jews should have a national homeland and, later, an independent state

Index